For Lauren, an amazing friend whose brilliant eye benefited
nearly every page of this book.

For Nate, whose steadfast love, support and sense of humor
not only got me through the daunting feeding journey,
but also proved beyond instrumental in bringing this book to life.

And for Olivia and Milo, the ultimate inspiration behind this story.

Edited by Ever After Studio, www.everafterstudio.com.
Book design by Tracy Sunrize Johnson.
Printed in China.

ISBN: 978-0-9864304-1-1

10 9 8 7 6 5 4 3 2 1

DynaMama LLC
527 Alvarado Street
San Francisco, CA 94114

DynaMama.com

The Places You'll Feed!

By Lauren Hirshfield Belden

Illustrated by Isabelle Angell

BROUGHT TO YOU BY

DYNAMAMA

The day has arrived!

Your baby has hatched.
Now comes the fun part—
Getting it latched!

There's milk in your boobs.
Your babe needs to eat.
It's time to get topless,
and offer a teat!

Grab your baby!
Your pillow!
And choose a position.
Try football or cradle—
Just use intuition.

You'll get loads of practice
from dawn through the night,
'til you're feeding while sleeping,
mixing left up with right.

Brewing teas, taking herbs
to perfect your supply.
Staining shirts, icing hurts,
you will laugh while you cry.

YES INDEED,
THE PLACES YOU'LL FEED!

See, feeding your babe,
well, it's not always pretty,
when you whip out a boob
in a cab in the city.

Or you crouch in the car
unzipping your dress,
ignoring the traffic,
deploring the stress—

Of the shrieking, the leaking,
the chaos galore,
as one boob sprays Baby,
the other the floor!

And speaking of floors...
it's time to commit
to making fast friends
with the places you'll sit.

To the dirt and the grime
and the dust and the rust,
and the nose-plugging smells
of the places you must
place your bottom upon
as you pull up your shirt,
bringing Baby to boob,
while you pray it won't hurt.

The tugging!
The sucking!
The biting, indeed!

OH, THE PLACES YOU'LL FEED!

And maybe your baby
won't take to the breast,
and you'll choose to spend hours
with pump strapped to your chest.

Through two plastic cones
and a bra with two holes,
you'll free up your hands
for other "big goals."

As you hook yourself up
to this pumping machine,
you may grimace and grumble
and say things obscene.

You'll plead with your nipples.
You'll beg them to squirt.
You'll stare at the clock
'til your eyes start to hurt.

And then when you've had
all you think you can take,
the sound of your pump
may just jolt you awake
with a song or a word
or a noise that's absurd,
but you'll swear that
your pump *spoke* that word that you heard!

Your pumping machine
likely came with a case,
which you'll find yourself dragging
all over the place.

You might set up your pump
at an airport gate,
while you pray that your flight
runs a little bit late.

You might drag it to work,
back and forth it will travel
from your home to your job
while your shoulders unravel.

DEPARTING!!

UP UP

AND AWAY

And many an office
just won't have a spot
that's not crowded
or freezing
or dreadfully hot
or spooky
or kooky
or full of computers
to hook up your pump
and squeeze milk from your hooters.

But the spot's got an outlet,
and that's all that you need...

GOOD GOD, THE PLACES YOU'LL FEED!

On a train!
On a plane!
At a game in the rain!

Out to eat!
On the street!
With your dogs at your feet!

At a club!
In the tub!
While you're cooking up grub!

By the pool!
Keeping cool!
Getting covered with drool!

By the sea!
On one knee!
Or the stump of a tree!

On a ride!
Side by side!
Where there's nowhere to hide!

And when you decide
you don't want to keep going,
your honkers have had it,
they're done with their flowing.
Let go of the guilt
with this life-changing thought:
Thank the Lord that good milk
can be easily bought!

And your baby will grow
drinking milk from the store,
and sleep like a champ
(or more than before).

You'll love it and hate it,
as you already know.
You'll hate it and love it—
This milk-making flow.

The bonding!
The fussing!
The cuddling!
The cussing!

And when you look back
on the lows and the highs—
The aching! The snuggling!
The locking of eyes!

The pumping and dumping!
The pain of un-lumping!
The pulse of your heart
when it really gets thumping—

This is one thought
That will never grow old...

You did it!
You've done it!
You made liquid gold!
Your baby is thriving!
It's a thing to behold.

AH, THE PLACES YOU'VE FED!